How to Trade Binary Options

Dana DeCecco

Dana is a former Commodity Trading Advisor

and 20 year independent trader

ISBN-13:978-1503257306

DEDICATION

This book is dedicated to the GOOD LORD who provides inspiration and imagination.

CONTENTS

ACKNOWLEDGMENTS

Charts by
Oanda FX
MT-4 Metatrader
FreeStockCharts.com

1 BINARY OPTIONS TRADING

Binary options are the latest addition to the asset trading game. The assets include stocks, futures, and forex. The trading process is simple but the process of trading is not.

Many Binary Options traders approach it as a gambling venture. That's OK if that is your goal. You will have a 50/50 chance of winning 80%. As far as I'm concerned, those odds stink. You will lose all of your money.

A little education goes a long way, notably with binary options, since the results are quick to come. You can get rich or poor very quickly. If you must guess, at least take an educated guess.

Before you trade, at least take the time to understand the game. The markets in general are subject to time tested laws, similar to the law of gravity. What goes up...must come down. OK, it's a little more complicated than that, but simple rules indicate much of binary option market movement.

Please take the time to learn and understand the simple concepts on this page. Binary option trading is the most simple form of trading market price action. If you learn about support, resistance and trends you will be way ahead of the pack. The best binary options systems and binary options signals are based on price action.

Binary Options trading is purely speculative. Although brokers refer to as investing, the primary purpose of Binary Options is to speculate on the price movement of certain assets. Select stocks, commodities, and forex pairs are the assets traded on the various platforms.

Binary options brokers earn money by creating a payout that is less than your original stake. Most brokers pay out 75 to 80% but some may pay up to 90%. The difference could be considered the spread.

Gambling on binary options is a losing proposition. A 75% return on your 50/50 chance is not a good return. You can get better odds at the casino.

Trading binary options is a different story. Using the proper techniques, you can actually get the odds in your favor. But only if you learn how to trade binary options. Binary Options Systems and Binary Options Signals will improve

Learn how to read a chart

Binary Options are a plain and simple way to trade based on your opinion of where a market is headed over a certain

period of time. They are contracts that pay out a predetermined amount or nothing at all at expiration. The payout amount for your option is determined before you place the trade.

Binary Options are based on an underlying security, commodity, or currency that have various strike prices to choose from as well as various expirations. Both call and put Binary Options are available for trading. If, at expiration, the price of the underlying security closes at or above the selected strike price, the buyer of a call Binary Option receives the payoff. If the underlying security closes at a price that is below the strike price on the expiration date, the buyer receives nothing.

In the case of put Binary Options, the put buyer receives the payoff per contract if the underlying security closes below the strike price at expiration, and nothing if the underlying security closes at or above the strike price at expiration.

The price of a Binary Option usually reflects the perceived probability that the underlying security price will reach or exceed (for call Binary Options) or fail to reach or exceed (for put Binary Options) the selected strike price at expiration. The cost of Binary Options will normally be quoted at a price per contract. The trader can buy multiple contracts. Buyers of Binary Options pay for the contract at the time of purchase. Binary Options are easy to trade but not easy to win. Learn how to trade binary options here. Binary Options systems are explained below.

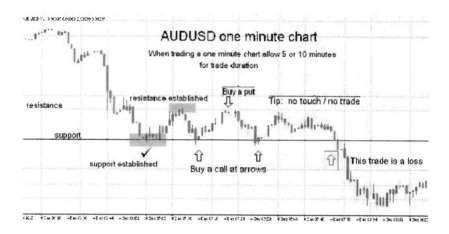

Reversal trading is my favorite Binary Options trading strategy. During the less volatile trading hours it can provide a very high degree of probability. As you can see on the chart above, 3 out of 4 trades were profitable. Trend trading as shown below is also a popular trading method.

Basic Technical Analysis Tips:

How to trade Binary Options

1) When viewing the price charts start with the higher time frame and work your way down to the time frame you are trading. Always look at the big picture even when trading one minute charts.

2) Draw SUPPORT and RESISTANCE lines on the chart that are near to the price point you are trading. These lines are drawn where the price has reversed direction in the past.

3) Draw TREND lines to show trends in all time frames or at least a few time frames.

The trend line indicates the general direction. The support and resistance lines are possible areas of a price reversal. Notice how the price action bounced off the the resistance level.

Dropping down to the one hour time frame we can clearly see that the trend is up. Trading is a game of probabilities. We use historical information (the price chart) to determine future probabilities. This chart tells us that the price will probably bounce off the trend line and head up toward the resistance line.

The 15 minute chart simply confirms our analysis. The price will not "always" behave as predicted. Our prediction is based on historical probability.

This 5 minute chart indicates a down trend in the short term. If the price action breaks through the long term trend line then it will probably continue down the short term trend line. Place a greater weight on the higher time frames when making a trading decision.

Buy a call. This is a reversal trade.

This one minute chart helps us to pinpoint the trade entry. This is actually a very good trade set up. I would buy a CALL on EURUSD but would not expect it to break through the resistance level above.

This method of trading is far superior to the "wild guess" method but requires a little homework. There are many technical ways to trade from a chart. This way is the simplest yet it is still the best. This analysis can be done on the broker supplied chart but it will not be nearly as accurate.

This is not a trade recommendation....It is simply how I trade. Support, Resistance, and Trends are the most important elements of trading. Binary options signals and binary option systems are based on basic technical analysis.

WARNING:

Trading futures, forex, stocks, and options involves the risk of loss. Please consider carefully whether futures, forex, stocks, or options are appropriate to your financial situation. Only risk capital should be used when trading. Investors could lose more than their original investment. You must review the customer account agreement prior to establishing an account. Past results are not indicative of future results. The risk of loss in trading can be substantial, carefully consider the inherent risks of such an investment in light of your financial condition.

All information on this website or any product purchased from this website is for educational purposes only and is not intended to provide financial advise. Any statements about profits or income, expressed or implied, does not represent a guarantee. Your actual trading may result in losses as no trading system is guaranteed.

Basic Option Trading

Once you get past the learning curve, option trading can open up a world of new trading strategies and trading systems. When I first began learning about options, it seemed very difficult and confusing. As I look back now, I don't recall what the confusion was all about. After all, there are only 4 basic option trades. All the other strategies are combinations of these 4 basic option trades.

As far as exchange traded options are concerned, we have calls and puts, and we can either buy or sell them. If you can learn and understand these 4 basic trades the complex strategies won't be hard at all. So, let's explore these 4 basic option trades.

When we buy an option, we have rights. We are paying the premium for these rights. If we buy a call, we have the right to buy the asset at the strike price we select,on or before expiration. If we buy a put, we have the right to sell the asset at the strike price we select, on or before expiration.

When we sell an option, we have obligations. Someone is paying us the premium for us to assume the obligation. If we sell a call, we have the obligation to sell the asset (to the person that bought the call) at the strike price we select, on or before expiration. If we sell a put, we have the obligation to buy the asset (from the person that bought the put) at the strike price we select, on or before expiration.

One advantage to trading options is that there does not need to be another person on the other side of the trade. I said it like that for illustrative purposes. The Options Clearing Corporation, which is a quasi-government organization, clears all exchange traded options. Therefore, if you are a buyer, you do not need a seller to make the trade. And if you are a seller, you do not need a buyer to make a trade. All transactions are completed immediately. The stock market does not work this way. Every seller needs a buyer, and every buyer needs a seller. Stock transactions generally take 3 days. There are many advantages to trading these derivatives. Contract expirations can be a liability to the buyer, and an asset to the seller. Learning to trade options will greatly enhance your trading arsenal.

Binary Options are much easier to trade than exchange traded options. The Binary Option trading platform just calls for one easy decision, UP or DOWN. My systems will help you make the CALL (or PUT).

Keeping it Simple

You got to work with what you got to work with. What we got to work with is Price, Time, and Volume. The universe of Technical Analysis is composed of these 3 elements. Every indicator, every system, and every strategy is comprised of these 3 elements. How many songs can be written with 3 notes? How many indicators can be conceived with 3 elements? Apparently, more than I can use. The key to successful technical analysis is simplicity. We have a tendency to complicate the issue. We think it can't be that simple. There must be a "Holy Grail" indicator. In our quest for the ultimate trading machine, we overlook the obvious.

When I open a price chart, I first view the chart with price and time only. Price and time will tell me everything I need to know. I can see volume playing out in price and time. I can see many popular indicators playing out in the price/time chart. I refer to the other indicators to confirm what I have just seen on the price chart. I often refer to Volume, Moving Averages, MACD, Stochastics, Bollinger Bands, and a few others to confirm what I already know. Reference to these indicators is a good thing. My initial analysis can sometimes be incorrect. I have good days and bad days. Indicators are good for keeping me focused on the price/time chart.

Fundamental analysis is a wonderful thing. It will most certainly complicate and confuse the issue. Most technicians believe the fundamentals are already on the chart. I am in this camp. I have, on many occasions, watched the price action on EUR/USD during the Non Farm Payroll release. I have seen price spike up 100 pips, then down 200 pips, then up 100 pips. In the end it generally ends up on the exact trendline it was following before the announcement.

You can take my advise and stick to the basics, or you can go ahead and complicate the heck out of it. I get the feeling that you are going to go ahead and complicate. That's what I did.

Advanced Trading
System Trading

Trading without a system is like driving with your eyes closed. Profitable trading is not possible without a system. Discretionary trading is a term that is misused. All trading is discretionary. It's always up to your discretion to enter or exit a trade, with or without a system. So what is a trading system? Well it is not: buy on the green light and sell on the red light. Some may make money using these systems, but some make money using slot machines in Vegas. A real trading system needs to be broken down into its individual components.

The first component in your trading system is your Money Management. This set of rules should always be observed. No discretion necessary. You need to decide how much you are willing to lose per trade. It's up to you to set these numbers. Let's say your initial trading account value is $2000. Of course, this is risk capital, money that you can afford to lose. With this amount of capital, I personally would be willing to lose 5% per trade. 5% of $2000 is $100.

If I am willing to lose $100 per trade, I should now know what kind of trades I can make. For example, I could buy one option contract for $100 or less. I could also trade a spot forex contract for $3 per pip, with a 33 pip stop loss. I could also buy 100 shares of a $5 stock if major support was at $4. Do you see how you work this backwards? First determine how much you are willing to lose per trade, then decide which asset you are going to trade.

The next component in our trading system is the trade. A trade has 3 components. The first is an entry. When and why will we enter this trade. What entry signal are we using? What is the anticipated profit and the maximum loss?

The second is a win exit. You must have a plan to exit the trade with a specified profit before you enter the trade.

The third is a loss exit. If your trade analysis is wrong, you should have a stop loss in place.

When you put this all together, you might have a system like this example. After my research and analysis, I have determined that EUR/USD will make a 100 pip move up, after this mornings economic release. I will enter a long position for $3 per pip as it bounces off the 50% Fibonacci level. My stop loss will be set at a 33 pip loss, and my take profit order will be set at a 100 pip sell stop order. I know from experience that I have a 50/50 chance of being successful. Once I place the trade, I can go outside and play. I know that when I return, I will have made $300 or lost$100 or the trade will still be in progress.

This,of course is a hypothetical trade and a hypothetical system. If you can develop a system that produces a 3 to 1 reward to risk ratio with a 50/50 chance of being correct, then you will become very wealthy.

Stochastic Trading System

The stochastics oscillator has been around for quite some time. This indicator is very reliable under certain conditions. It does not work well in trending markets. If the market is moving in a sideways or consolidating pattern the indicator can be very predictive.

Above is a one minute chart of the Nasdaq 100. The buy signal occurs when the indicator crosses up through 20 and the sell signal occurs when the indicator crosses down through 80.

It is best to trade this system during quiet market hours. For example, the EURUSD forex pair is quiet after the closing of

New York market hours at 4pm EST (GMT-5). During this time EURUSD normally oscillates up and down in a sideways channel.

Be sure to set the indicator in conjunction with the time frame you are trading. I use the settings of 14/3/3 but you can experiment and see what is working at the time you are trading.

Divergence System Example

The MACD indicator measures the difference between moving averages. It is one of the classic indicators.

Divergence is an anomaly that indicates something is wrong. If MACD is telling you the price should be giong lower but the price is going higher then something has to give,

There are many variations on this system and it also works well with stochastics. Here is an example :

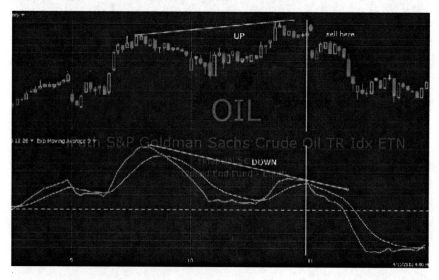

This is a 15 minute chart of the ETF OIL. The ETF will track the commodity.

If you are using an indicator on a 15 minute chart you should be trading on an hourly time frame. This chart will do you no good on a one minute trade.

Parabolic SAR trading system

Parabolic SAR (SUPPORT and RESISTANCE) is an indicator that could be considered a trading system in itself. When the indicator dots jump from over to under, the price will normally change direction.

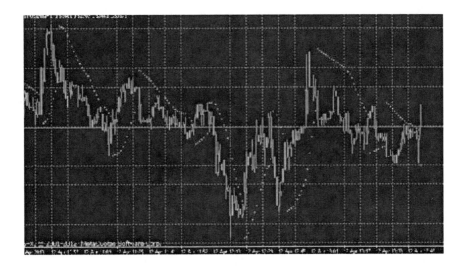

This is a one minute chart of GBPUSD. Notice the wild candles on the right. Extremely high volatility is expected during economic announcements !

For the 60 second trader, free 5 and 10 second charts are available by opening a practice account with Oanda FX. Although I do not recommend 60 second trading.

Martingale System for Binary Options :

The Martingale system was developed for casino gambling where the payout percentage is closer to even money. The rules are simple. Just double your bet each time you lose. Sooner or later you will win and cover all losses with a small profit.

The Martingale system does not work as well with Binary Options. The payout is closer to 75% so each time you lose you must triple your bet. This method could get very expensive. Let's try an example with an initial bet of only one dollar.

bet $1   loss = $1
bet $3   loss = $4   or   win = $5.25
bet $9   loss = $14   or   win = $15.75
bet $27   loss = $41   or   win = $47.25
bet $81   loss = $122   or   win = $141.75

Can you lose 5 times in a row ? Of course you can. How deep are your pockets ? There is no table limit with binary options

2 Trading Examples

Before trading binary options you should be aware of the potential risks and rewards. The online extremists are either overly bullish or bearish on the subject. But there is middle ground.

Binary options are the latest trading venue on the market. Everybody wants a piece of the pie including the regulated US exchanges. Just like every other form of asset trading, binary options can be approached as a gambling venture or as a trading venture. In either case they are definitely not an approach to investing in any way. Binary trading is not investing.

Binary options probably attract more gamblers than traders. Unfortunately, the odds are terrible. You have a 50/50 chance of profiting 75% of your bet. Any casino gambler worth their weight will tell you those odds are heavily weighted against you. Any casino game will offer better odds than that. The numerous online complaints about offshore brokers are probably from gamblers since most traders know what they are getting into.

The USA offers a line of binary options on the exchanges such as the CBOE and NADEX. Offshore brokers are numerous and new brokers seem to be popping up daily. Many are legitimate and some are working with the US exchanges to gain access. Sooner or later they will probably gain access to the lucrative US market.

Many binary option brokers offer sign up bonus money. You won't get the money until you trade a designated amount of trading volume. This could be considered good news for traders and bad news for gamblers. In any case, the brokers are not in business to give away money. Trading signals are offered by some brokers and can be used as confirmation for your own market analysis.

The good news is that binary options are very easy to trade. Novice traders can easily negotiate the platform. The simplicity of the trade is a very attractive feature and the trading platforms are user friendly and well designed. The brokers and associates are helpful and friendly but then again most salesmen are.

Binary options may be easy to trade but they are not easy to win. A little education will go a long way for anyone considering this kind of option trading. Consider the fact that you need to win 3 out of 5 trades to overcome the risk/reward ratio. You better get your game on before entering the playing field.

With the right training, binary options can be traded with success on a regular basis. There are trading techniques that are well suited for binary option trading. These basic strategies can be learned in a very short period of time and are the same trading systems used by professional traders. They are fundamental and timeless.

Before risking your money get the odds in your favor and learn basic chart analysis. The 75% payout doesn't look too bad if the odds are in your favor. If your gambling, forget about it.

These chart images were captured at the same moment in time. First analyze the big picture and work your way down to the one minute time frame. I use the free MT4 charting platform.

GBPUSD daily chart

The trend is bullish

The daily trend is bullish.

Trend line down

Trend line break = bullish

GBPUSD hourly chart

The hourly trend is bearish but the trend line break is a bullish signal.

The breakout through resistance is a bullish indicator.

The price was unable to break through support. Buy a call.

All time frames are bullish. This is a high probability trade.

Here is a quick start guide just to give you the general idea:

This is where we explain how you can make money trading binary options. We will show you how to increase your odds from 50% to 80%. Trading is all about probabilities. Some trades have a higher probability of success than others. You can put the odds in your favor if you follow this simple technique.

STEP 1 - Find an asset that exhibits one of the following conditions:

* trending up or down
* near support or
* near resistance

Study the charts below to understand the concepts of trend, support, and resistance. They are the absolute most important factors used by professional traders. Learning these simple concepts will enable you to trade with success.

The red line on the chart below indicates an upward trend. Notice how the price continues to bounce off the red line. When the price pulls back to the trend line you would buy a call expecting the price to continue on the upward trend. Always allow enough time for the trade to work. We are viewing a one hour chart so 10 or 15 minutes should be enough time. 60 second trading is not suitable for analysis at all, in fact it is more like gambling than trading.

During a downward trend you would apply the same principle in reverse and buy a put, expecting the asset to continue on a downward trend.

Although trend trading is heavily promoted, it is not a good way to trade binary options. Reversal trading is a better style and more suited to binary option trading.

The TREND is your friend until the end. So, when does the trend end ? The trend comes to an end when it encounters SUPPORT or RESISTANCE.

The red line on the chart below represents a SUPPORT line. It is a price point that the asset value has bounced off in the past. Price action tends to reverse direction when it encounters a support area. This is known as a reversal strategy. You would buy a call when the price is sitting on support.

We are looking for HIGH PROBABILITY trades. The price will be repelled by support or resistance with a high degree of probability. BUT NOT EVERY TIME. You will have losing trades. The idea is to have more winners than losers. I have been trading for 15 years at a professional level and still have my share of losing trades but my winners outnumber the losers ending up net profitable.

The final chart in our brief tutorial is RESISTANCE. Price action tends to reverse direction when it encounters resistance. It is the opposite of support and you would buy a put expecting the price to pull back. AS you can clearly see, the price has pulled back from this area in the past and is likely to do so in the future.

Be patient and wait for the best trades. You don't need to be trading all the time. The key to trading is timing the market. Initiate the trade at the right time and allow enough time for the price to move in the direction of your trade.

WHY IS THIS TRADING STRATEGY SO SIMPLE ?

The laws of supply and demand determine the daily fluctuation in asset prices.

Assets can be considered undervalued or overvalued by traders causing the price to bounce between the extremes.

As the price assumes a directional bias more and more traders jump on the bandwagon to get a piece of the action.

The rally (or trend) will finally exhaust itself running out of buyers or sellers and creating a price reversal.

This kind of price action will continue until it has a reason to break through support or resistance or reverse from these levels.

Be careful trading during news related announcements.

Under normal trading conditions the trend and reversal strategies are very high probability trades.

This is very important information. Why are you sharing it for free?

It is the traders that drive the price action. The more traders using a system - the better it works ! The markets we are trading are huge and there is more than enough volume to allow the home based trader to accumulate wealth. Over the past few years, home based trading has grown exponentially due to the high tech trading platforms available to us today. Modern technology has leveled the playing field ! You can effectively compete with the Wall Street traders.

They say a picture is worth a thousand words

EURUSD 1 minute chart

resistance

support

Any Questions ?

Q - 1. What makes Binary Options different ?

Generally, the pricing for Binary Options versus traditional options is different, reflecting the fact that Binary Options pay out a fixed amount whereas traditional options' value (or payout) increases as the underlying increases.

Q - 2. Can I sell my Binary Option before expiration?

Usually. If you sell your option for more than you paid for it, you will collect the difference.

Q - 3. What if the underlying closes above my selected strike price prior to expiration? For a call...............

The underlying needs to close at or above your selected strike price at expiration time to trigger the payout. A closing price above your strike price before expiration has no affect on the contract and does not trigger a payout.

Q - 4. What if the underlying closes AT the strike price?

Brokers will return your investment if the trade breaks even.

Q - 5. Where do Binary Options trade?

A reputable Binary Options broker is listed on this website. Binary Options are traded over the counter.

Q - 6. How are Binary Options priced?

In general, the prices quoted for Binary Options will reflect the market's perceived probability that the underlying security will close at or above the strike price, in the case of Calls (or below the strike price in the case of Puts).

Q - 7. How is the settlement price determined?

Your broker will post the payout before you make the trade. The settlement price for Binary Options is determined by the equation used by your broker.

EURUSD 1 minute chart

Timing is the key   60 second trading is a loser

resistance

support

Patience is your best friend. Timing is everything. WAIT FOR THE GOOD TRADES. Fools rush in.

If you could make only one trade per day you would wait for a very promising one. This is how you should trade.

This trade was a winner, perfect timing. The next is a set up for a loser. I made the trade before the price hit the resistance line because the time clock was running out. Big mistake, I know better. Do not make the trade unless conditions are just right.

I entered this trade prematurely. The price must first bounce off the resistance line. I bought a put and the price went higher. It is very easy to get anxious and hurry the trade, even for an old pro like me. Can you learn from my mistake ?

Support / Resistance level showing various trade entry points.

DISCLAIMER:
Trading futures, forex, stocks, and options involves the risk of loss. Please consider carefully whether futures, forex, stocks, or options are appropriate to your financial situation. Only risk capital should be used when trading. Investors could lose more than their original investment. You must review the customer account agreement prior to establishing an account. Past results are not indicative of future results. The risk of loss in trading can be substantial, carefully consider the inherent risks of such an investment in light of your financial condition.

All information on this website or any product purchased from this website is for educational purposes only and is not intended to provide financial advise. Any statements about profits or income, expressed or implied, does not represent a guarantee. Your actual trading may result in losses as no trading system is guaranteed.

3 Basics

A step by step guide for beginners. I will show you how to trade Binary Options and spot FOREX.

I am a veteran trader. I know how to trade stocks, options, futures, and forex just to name a few. It would take many years for you to learn these skills. Binary Options is the simplest form of trading but it is not easy to win.

I can teach you how to trade a portion of this market if you are willing to do what I tell you. Below is a step by step guide for you to follow. There is no easy way! Forget the signals. They are useless if you do not know how to trade. Binary options for beginners could be called Forex for beginners because we are trading forex.

Do not believe Signal Providers that tell you it is easy. They are lying. The short course in trading that follows is the easiest and fastest way to learn this business. We will focus on Forex because the charting apps are easy to get and superior to stock charts.

RULES:
1) Money Management
Trade only with money you can afford to lose. My personal rule for trade value is 5% of the account value. With a $1000 trading account , I would trade no more than $50 on each trade. For smaller accounts you will have to go with 10% max.

2) Slow Down

We are never in a hurry to get into a trade. Trades are like busses...another will be along soon. There is no rule saying that you have to be in a trade. If the set-up doesn't jump off the chart screaming FREE MONEY, then don't take the trade.

3)Pick Your time

Reversal trading works best during quiet market hours because it takes the big gorilla to push the market through a support or resistance line. The big gorilla normally trades near the London and New York open and during economic announcements.

4) Asset Selection

We don't trade everything and anything because different assets do not react the same. Pick a few and get to know them. Forex is a good choice because the charts are free and superior to other assets.

5) Be Afraid

The water is full of sharks. Enter the market cautiously because no matter how good the system is you will still lose trades. That's why we trade the same amount on every trade. When you bet the farm you will probably lose.

6) Don't get greedy

As the old market saying goes "pigs get slautered". The big gorilla will allow you to make a reasonable return but.........

7) Don't trust your broker

Most of the employees at the brokerage (including US brokers) don't know anything about trading. As far as Binary Options brokers it's even worse than that. Make sure you get paid. Select your broker wisely.

The websites offering broker comparisons are full of Sh*!

8) Test your broker

Before dumping twenty grand into an account, start out small. Open a smaller size account and try withdrawing some of your funds. Make sure you are not having any problem getting your money. Some of these Binary Options brokers have very little cash behind them and they are counting on you to lose all of your money.

9) The "force" is not with you

You better get your game on. To maintain profitability you need to win 3 out of 5 trades. Easier said than done, even with a good system. If you don't know everything I am teaching you on this page, then DON'T TRADE. You will eventually lose all of your money.

10) This is a universal system

No matter what you are trading (stocks, options, futures, forex) this system will work for you. It is based on universal laws of motion in the financial markets. I know this from experience. I hope you take my word for it because it took me many, many years sifting through the mountain of bullshit on the internet. If you spend 10 years researching systems you will eventually end up back on this page.

Tools of the Trade

You need tools just like a carpenter needs a hammer and saw. You can try trading from the Binary Options Brokers chart and may have some success. Support and resistance levels are visible on a short term horizon. I have checked out the accuracy of many broker charts and found them to be very accurate. But most of their charts are not interactive and the larger time-frames are essential for high probability trades.

I would never trade using the broker supplied charts. I trade from the MT4 platform and only use the broker site to enter orders. This presents a problem for lazy traders and those that think they can successfully trade from a cell phone. I guess its possible but you still need to have the 2 programs running unless you are making long term trades.

The MT4 charting platform is free. You can open a practice account with any number of MT4 brokers .

You should also have a desktop shortcut to Forex Factory. An economic announcement calendar is on this site. These are the times not to trade unless you like to gamble. There are ways to trade the news profitably but I'm not going to cover them in this book.

Now that we have our charting analysis platform, we are going to draw lines. I know you have eyes, but draw the lines anyhow.

We are going to draw lines because we will check them out in various time frames.

TIP:

The higher the time-frame the more reliable the S/R line will be. (S/R is support/resistance). A support line on a DAILY chart is far more reliable than on a 5 minute chart. This is why the broker supplied charts fall short. They know that, and many of them want you to lose your money because they are not hedging your trade like they should. You lose / they win.

How to Find a Trade

Before you go searching for a trade open your brokers platform and let it run in the background. If you find a great opportunity you want to be ready to push the button. UP is a CALL and DOWN is a PUT. Pre-set your trade amount if possible and set up the currency pairs you are looking at. Don't try to be an expert at everything. Better to be an expert at one pair than a well rounded loser. There are many times when I turn on my laptop and find no trades at all.

TIP:

The asset you are trading must be AT or NEAR a S/R line. If it is near the line then you wait for the trade to develop. Trading is ALL about waiting. You trade like a predator, waiting for the precise moment to make your move. This is the hardest part for all of us. But you will lose if you do not acquire this skill. Patience separates the pros from the rookies.

If you spot a trade and you are a little late.....forget about it.

Move on to the next search. It will drive you crazy but you must get the timing together. Binary Option trading is all about TIMING unlike spot forex trading. That is why it is hard.

This looks like a promising opportunity. One bounce off resistance on the 5 minute chart.

DRAW THE LINE

Do not be in a hurry, ever.

Let's see what it looks like on a higher time-frame. The 15 minute and 1 hour charts produced no results.

EUR/USD 4 hour chart

Binary Options are a plain and simple way to trade based on your opinion of where a market is headed over a certain period of time. They are contracts that pay out a pre-determined amount or nothing at all at expiration. The payout amount for your option is determined before

This 4 hour chart looks real good. There has been a lot of activity right on our S/R line.

Let's go up one more time-frame. Once you get the hang of it, this process takes less than a minute.

This is a major S/R line

EUR/USD Daily chart

The daily chart confirms our trade. Look at the action on this line. You only had to draw one line.

This is MAJOR S/R

I would take the trade and buy a PUT on EUR/USD with a 10 or 15 minute expiry. 2 or 3 minutes may not be enough time for the price to bounce.

When is the exact right time? That is a very hard question for me to answer because the art of trading is not always based on mathematical equations. If it were that simple we could program a computer to do it. And, in fact, we have. Program trading accounts for a very large percentage of trade volume, on some days exceeding 80%. All the players are not on the same page resulting in erratic price movement that defies logic.

Please understand, I have well over 100,000 hours of trading experience. I have studied a million charts and made thousands of trades, real and hypothetical. I can't give you my experience. The best I can do is provide examples and commentary on trading situations. You will have to pay your dues to join the club.

TIP:

 Binary Options Traders use 1 minute and 5 minute signals unless trading a longer term option. Forex Day Traders use 5 minute and 15 minute signals

TIP:

Set your charts up on the MT4. Always use SUPPORT and RESISTANCE lines
A signal near one of these lines creates a very high probability trade
These trades are REVERSAL trades

EUR/USD 1 hour chart with support line drawn

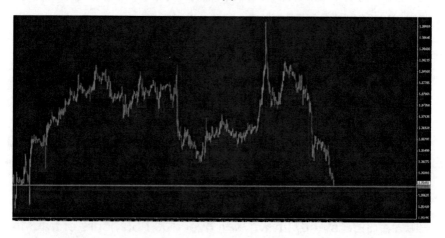

USD/CAD 30 minute chart with resistance line set. The strength of a S/R line is determined by the price reversals on the larger time-frames. A daily chart carries more weight than a 5 minute chart.

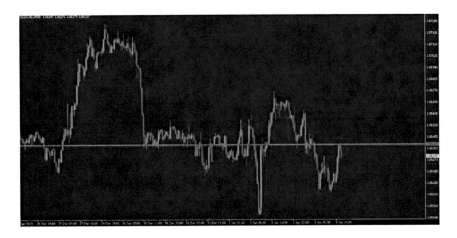

Using my reversal trading system will make you a very powerful trader.

The single other factor of great importance is TIMING. You may have to practice awhile to get the timing together.

That is why a 15 minute signal is not good for a 5 minute expiration. The time frame is too great for the trade.

I can't help you with timing. It comes with experience.

Reversal trading is better suited for binary options than trend trading. Trend indicators are too slow for fast paced binary option trading.

Pullbacks must be identified to day trade trends. Indicators will fall short due to their lagging nature.

Binary options signals and forex signals will not make you a winning trader. You must first learn how to trade to use the signals.

Learn to Trade Divergence

This is a chart pattern based system, combined with the moving average convergence - divergence indicator. It is the easiest to implement of all the forex systems I use.

Actually we are searching mainly the 15 minute time frame charts for "double tops" and "double bottoms", with a MACD divergence.

MACD is an indicator available on ALL charting programs. I simply use the standard settings of 12,26,9. It will already be set up this way. 15 minute time frame charts are also available on ALL charting programs.
So, lets move on to a chart:

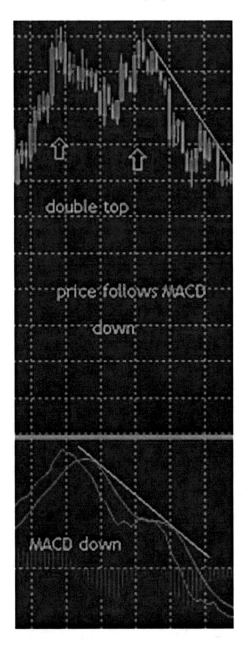

This chart displays a double top pattern. The tops must be even (or very close).

As you can see, while the price was forming the second top,

the MACD indicator was on a downhill ride. We would place a trade to sell (go short) near the 2nd yellow up arrow. The price follows the MACD down. Our bank account goes up.

This is an easy trade to find and an easy trade to make.

This trade is 80% accurate. No trade is 100% accurate.

Next is a chart of an almost perfect double bottom. The yellow arrows point to the double bottoms. We would enter a LONG POSITION (buy) after the second arrow.

MACD has bottomed out on the first yellow arrow and then began a consistent upward move. The price formed a second bottom WITHOUT the confirmation of MACD.

If the double bottom is on a SUPPORT line, this would give

us a very good confirmation to make the trade.

If price would make a sharp turn down after we enter the trade and break through support, we would exit the trade and take a small loss. You WILL have losses. Try to keep them small and let the winners run. You will win or lose on a Binary Option trade.

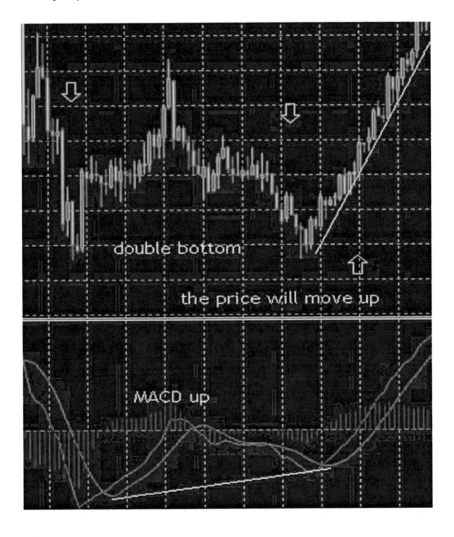

.WOW ! Check this baby out.

This is a perfect double bottom. It landed dead on support.

Look how the price runs away after the second touchdown !

This is the trade we search for. It occurs nearly every day in one of the major pairs. One of these trades a week is all you need to profit in the business of online trading.

This all looks very easy, but in the heat of battle your emotions may distort your logic. Never trade without a system. A trading system has rules.
You must abide by the rules without emotion. That is why we trade only with RISK CAPITAL. That is money you can afford to lose.
Trading is a game. Sometimes you win, sometimes you lose. The object of the game is to win big and lose small.

Trading without a plan (system) is like driving a car with your eyes closed. Know your plan BEFORE you make the trade.

FOREX trading checklist:
1) Know your brokers trading platform. Open a practice account and learn margin rules, order entry, trade exit, charting, and everything about the platform you are using.
2) Determine how much money you are willing to LOSE on each trade. If you are willing to lose 5% and your account balance is $1000, then you can afford to lose $50 on an individual trade. If you are trading for $1 per pip, then your

stop loss should be set at 50 pips or less.

3) Before entering a trade you must determine when to get in and when you are getting out. I normally use technical analysis to determine my entry and exit points.

Trading may appear to be easy, but it is not easy. I have been trading for 15+ years and still work everyday to refine my systems and tactics. The markets are constantly changing.

Double tops and bottoms can be found in all markets, such as forex, futures, and stocks. They can also be found in all timeframes, such as 5 min,15 min, 1 hour, and daily. The longer the timeframe, the longer the trade will take.

Don't let the simplicity of this system fool you. It is one of the most dependable systems I trade.

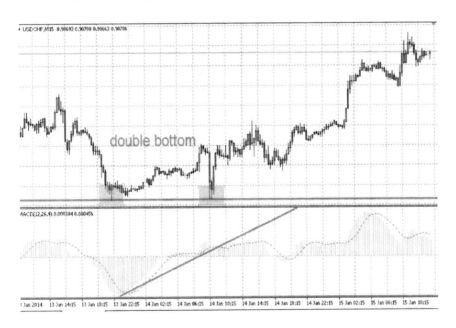

4 Trading Nadex

Nadex is a US regulated broker and the only broker that I actually trust. After all, if the offshore brokers refuse to pay you, what are going to do about it?

We use the same binary options system to trade on the Nadex platform. Use the same MT4 charts. I will cover Forex trading on the Nadex Binary Options platform because our signals are based on currency pair trading. Learning how to trade Nadex is simple.

Here is an image of their platform.

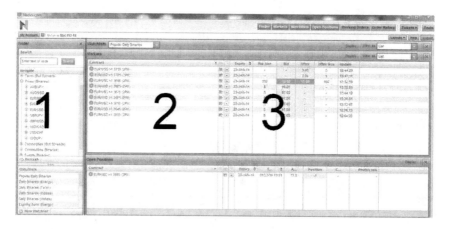

Placing a trade is easy as 1-2-3.

1) These are the forex pairs available to trade on the Nadex binary options platform.

Just click to open a pair and see which contracts are currently available.

The more heavily traded pairs will offer more contracts.

Certain contracts trade at different times of day and some longer term contracts can be traded anytime.

```
⊟ Forex (Binaries)
   ⊞ AUD/JPY
   ⊞ AUD/USD
   ⊞ EUR/GBP
   ⊞ EUR/JPY
   ⊞ EUR/USD
   ⊞ GBP/JPY
   ⊞ GBP/USD
   ⊞ USD/CAD
   ⊞ USD/CHF
   ⊞ USD/JPY
```

Different times of day will show different contracts times. Nadex trades 24/5
For example, the 1pm to 3pm contract can only be traded during that time period. The Daily(7pm) can be traded anytime during the day up untill the 7pm expiration.
The weekly contract can be traded anytime during the week up untill closing on Friday.

2) This provides a pretty good variety of short and long term contracts.

Click on a contract and the strike prices will show in the CONTRACT window.

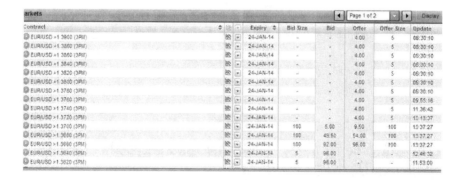

These are the daily contracts on EUR/USD due to expire at 3pm today. The strike prices are in the first column. Then the expiry and prices. For starters, these are the 3 things to learn and really all you need to know to place a trade.

Notice the strike prices:
>   EUR/USD> 1.3680 (at 3pm today)

If you buy this contract, you are buying a CALL at a strike price of 1.3680 so the price of EUR/USD must be higher than 1.3680 at 3pm today for you to win.

If you sell this contract, you are buying a PUT at a strike price of 1.3680 so the price of EUR/USD must be lower than 1.3680 at 3pm today for you to win.

3) This is the BID / OFFER window

click on OFFER to BUY the contract (buy a call)

click on BID to sell the contract (buy a put)

The difference in prices is the SPREAD. That is how the broker makes money. It doesn't matter whether you win or lose because Nadex makes the spread. Nadex hopes you win so that you keep trading.
Unlike some other Binary Options brokers , Nadex is not on the other side of your trade. Your trade is guaranteed by the Options Clearing Corporation which guarantees payment on all option trades in the US.

The bottom line is that NADEX collects thier fee when you place the trade.

Don't get confused over the bid and offer. Just click:
OFFER =the future price will be higher
BID = the future price will be lower

Bid	Offer
-	5.00
-	5.00
-	5.00
2.00	7.50
6.00	11.50
11.50	17.50
19.50	25.50
29.50	36.00
41.00	48.00
53.50	60.00
65.00	71.50
75.50	81.50
83.50	89.00
89.00	94.50
93.00	98.50

If you learn how to trade Nadex you will have a reliable broker.

When you click on the bid or offer the TICKET will pop up, just enter how many contracts you want and click place order.

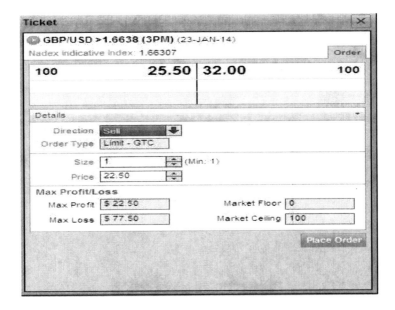

The OPEN POSITIONS window keeps track of your PROFIT
or LOSS in real time. You can close out your position at any
time to capture profits or cut losses.

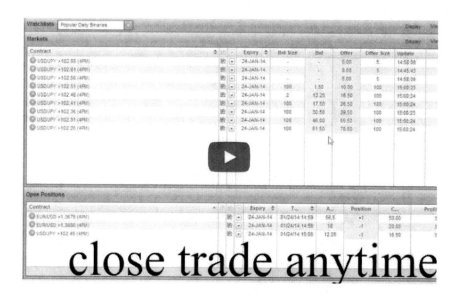

5 Trading Naked

How to Trade with Charts

How to trade stocks, commodities, forex, or anything with a chart.

No signals, no indicators, just you and the chart. Naked !

Once you learn basic charting methods you can trade almost any asset. Stocks, commodities and forex are nearly the same when it comes to technical analysis. Of course there are differences but the fundamental chart reading techniques remain the same. This is about how to trade with charts only.

Your primary method of trading should not include signals or indicators. Trading signals and indicators should be used to confirm what you already see or to alert you to a possible trade set-up. Without the basic chart reading skills the signals and indicator based systems will yield poor results.

The signals and indicators will not help if you don't know how to use them. Indicators can be misleading and even the best signals will fail. Basic charting is easy to learn and the basics are the most essential elements to successful trading.

Learn when and how to employ signals and indicators to enhance your charting skills.

Above all else is SUPPORT AND RESISTANCE. Resistance is a point above the current price where the price has stalled and changed direction in the past. Support is a point below the current price where the price has changed direction in the past.

A S/R (support/resistance) line on a daily chart carries more weight than a S/R line on an hourly chart. A S/R line on a 15 minute chart carries more weight than a S/R line on a one minute chart.

Why are these lines so important? I do not know. I just know that they are and that is all I need to know. They are price points that are plugged in to some giant trading computers used by Central Banks, Market Makers, Trading Syndicates,

Governments?

Many of these S/R lines go back for years and years. See my Holy Grail Youtube video. No other thing is more important for a trader to understand. You could profitably trade with just using S/R lines!

Always draw lines, and do it in different time-frames. Charts like the one I used above are common. It took me one minute to find this chart. This is the reality of trading. If you are not using S/R lines then you will fail.

Only 3 types of markets:

TRENDING UP

TRENDING DOWN

TRADING WITHIN A RANGE

That's it....it's either going up, down, or ranging

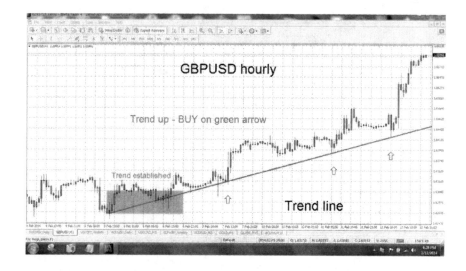

Trending occurs on the way to support or resistance. During the bullish trend above the price will stall, reverse direction or correct when it encounters resistance The price never moves in a straight line. It will always correct and exhibit a Fibonacci retracement. The price will retrace a certain percentage of the move.

We don't know how long the trend will last. Major resistance levels can be found on the higher time-frames. The price will have a more difficult time pushing through the major resistance levels. This is normally accomplished during volatile market hours when the big players are trading.

That is why or signals are best traded during quiet market hours. There is not enough pressure to push through the S/R levels resulting in a higher probability of a reversal.

Notice that we draw the trend line above a down trend and below the up trend. Trends occur in all time-frames. The expiration of your Binary Options trade will determine the time frame you are viewing. The 4 hour trend above will be useless on a 10 minute trade. Short term traders should be using the 1 and 5 minute time-frames.

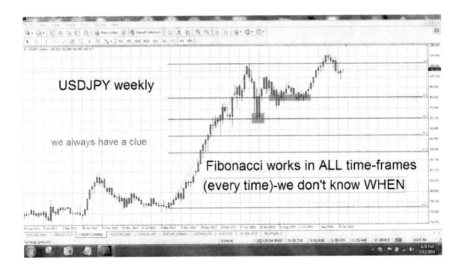

Market corrections or "Fibonacci Retracements" occur in all

markets and in all time-frames. There is no explanation for this anomaly but it happens 100% of the time and it is very accurate. We know it WILL happen but we we do not know WHEN it will happen or to what extent. Our trading signals are based on Fibonacci relationships.

Learn how to use the Fibo tool. It is provided free on every charting package.

You can trade strong currencies against weak currencies using this free site.

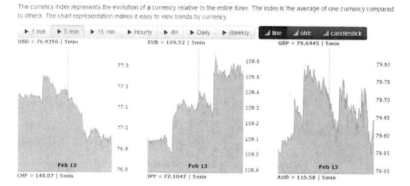

Go to **mataf.net**

Be careful trading during economic announcements.

Go to **ForexFactory.com**

Believe it or not, you can trade successfully if you just learn the information provided in this chapter.

- Support and resistance
- Trends
- Drawing lines on the chart
- Fibonacci
- Currency strength
- Economic calendar

Signals are great for giving you a "heads up". Indicators are good for confirmation and divergence systems. Chart patterns and candlestick patterns are also very good indicators. I can't explain all these in this book.

Learn the basics until it becomes second nature then add all the bells and whistles you want. After you search for the ultimate indicator for 10 years, you will come back to the basics. There is no ultimate indicator, secret system, magic guru, super duper signal, or holy grail.

Just you and the chart.

CPSIA information can be obtained at www.ICGtesting.com
Printed in the USA
LVOW10s1737120115

422499LV00002B/394/P